No More Crutch

Written by:
Jason Insalaco

Copyright © 2012
ISBN#978-1469995625
146999562X

INSTINCTIVE BIRD™

www.instinctivebird.com

Preface

In 1995 I was diagnosed with Bipolar Disorder. Before my diagnosis I used to abuse drugs and alcohol to escape the symptoms of an illness that didn't have a name. When I was diagnosed, I started writing to keep track of my feelings and thoughts. This book is a collection of these writings which took place from the early years of my ongoing recovery.

Looking at a weakness could be looked at like a test. A weakness can be transformed to an incredible strength. I've found if you use your weakness as a gift, it can turn out to be a blessing in disguise.

2 Corinthians 12:9
Contemporary English Version
But he replied, "My gift of undeserved grace is all you need. My power is strongest when you are weak." So if Christ keeps giving me his power, I will gladly brag about how weak I am.

Dedication

This book of writings is dedicated to the family
and friends who were there to support me
during my hard times in recovery.
Learning from my past,
Keeps me in today,
And shows me endless possibilities for my
future.
To my beautiful wife and children who see me
as I am today,
You are truly my life and my future.

Through ups and downs,
comes adversity.
Through adversity,
Comes wisdom.
Through wisdom,
Comes prosperity.

EXPERIENCE LIFE

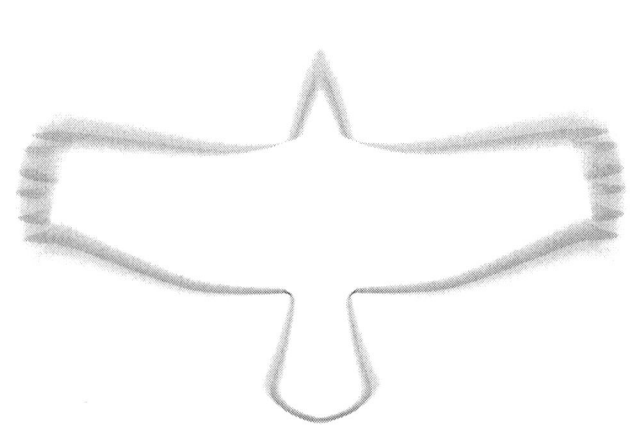

Time to come together,
No more fear from the differences.
It's all the same.
Come out of your shells.
Confront your fears.
Out of Darkness, I will shine.

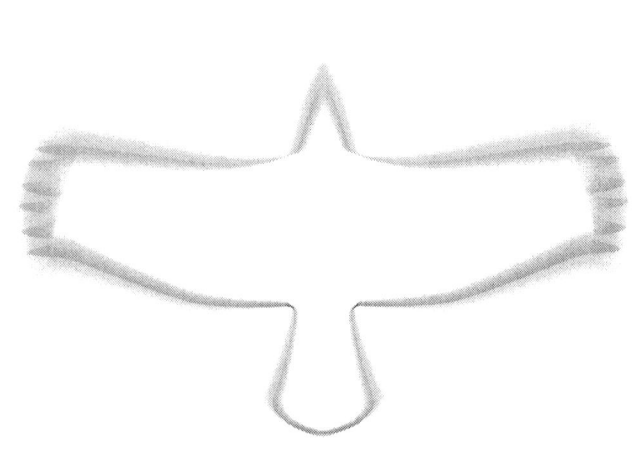

…a walk through recovery

Death in your eyes,
Blank stare cries,
Not in touch,
No more crutch.
RECOVERY

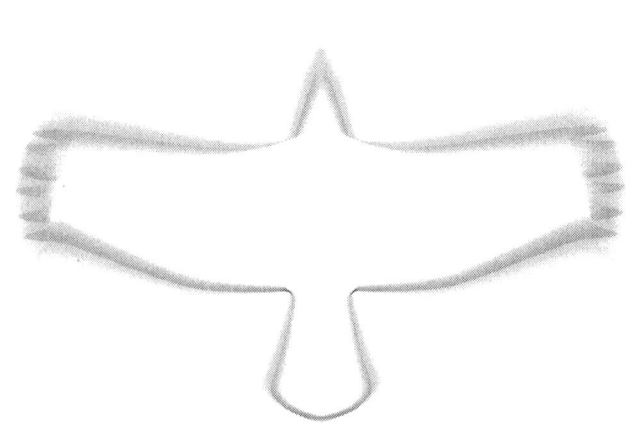

FORCE

Sometimes you're forced to do things against your will.
Don't worry, they're just stones to kick aside to let you grow spiritually.
Don't run, hide, and turn your back, your problems don't go away.
Look up and see your answers for what they are.
Realize the purpose.
Learn your lessons.
Answer your questions,
For I will always be by your side.

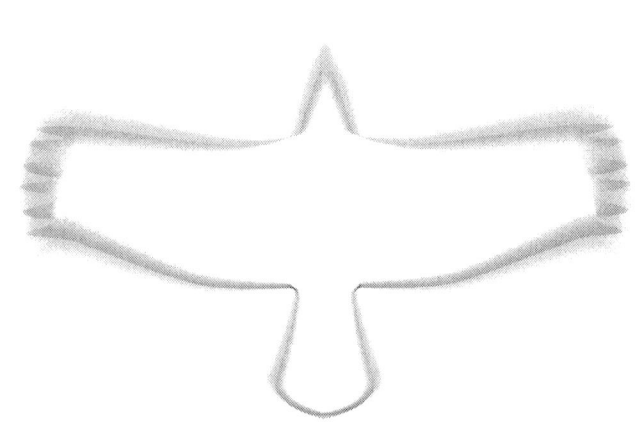

REAL

No more fake emotions.
It's time to feel for real.
Passing off the unrealities of life.
You'll never prosper with these phony feelings.
KEEP IT REAL
Go with the pain and feel the lesson.
Deal with the pain to bring you to the next level.
FEEL THEN DEAL

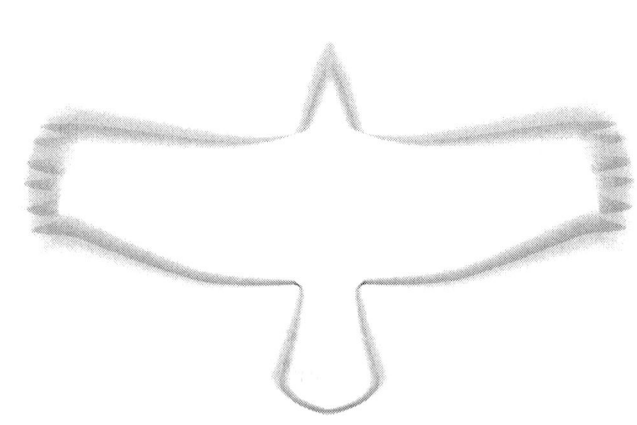

MAKE A CHOICE

Looking for the answers,
Just run away,
Nowhere to go,
Nowhere to hide.
Looking for the key to the ignorance you have
deep inside.
Look inside you'll see the answers,
Trust yourself and let yourself go.
You have to be strong to do the right thing.
Now it's time to,
MAKE A CHOICE

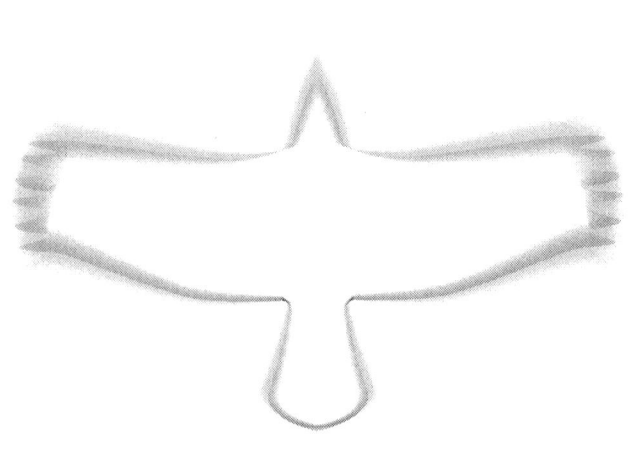

DEAL WITH THIS

It's all bottled tight and ready to explode.
Never showing your true feelings,
Wondering why you feel alone.
It's time to let it out and show who you really are,
It's all bottled tight and ready to explode.
Sometimes you have to scream to let it out,
Sometimes you have to sit down and think it out.
I was never taught to deal with this.
Need a release to keep me sane,
To deal with all this unseen pain.

DEAL WITH THIS

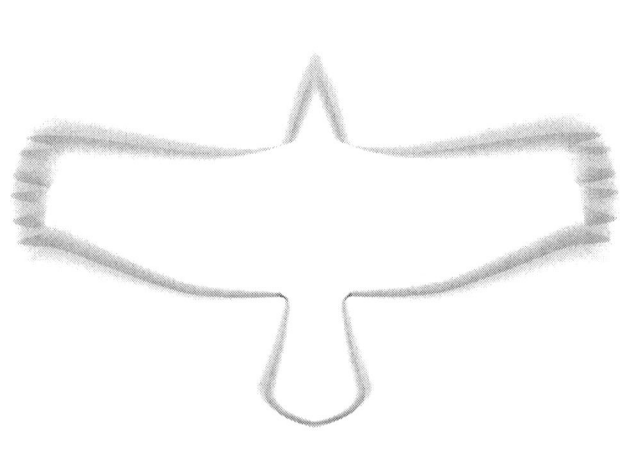

RUNAROUND

Blame the world for everything,
Why not blame me?
Ignorance is running you in circles.
Get a grip, get control.
Pull yourself to the surface,
You're in too deep!
HELP!
I'm drowning in all these lies.
I need your help to satisfy.
Look to the sky for answers,
Look to the sun,
You'll find you're not the only one.
It's time to take charge of your life,
Do it out of spite.
Show them what you have on the inside.
Wise up and be yourself,
They're giving you the RUNAROUND.

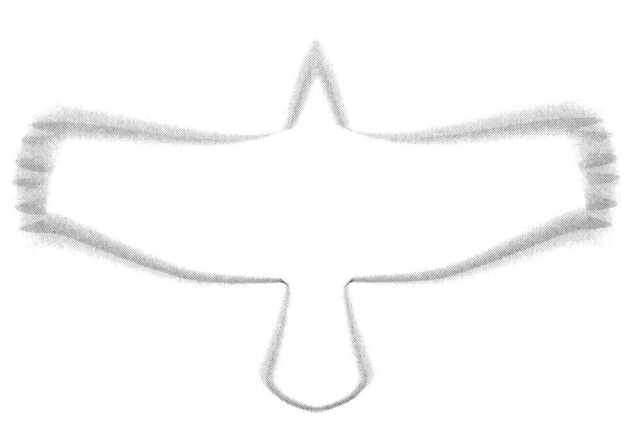

CHANGE?

What's today?
It's all the same,
All mundane,
It has to change.
Everyone and everything is still the same,
Feels the same,
When's the change?
It has to change.

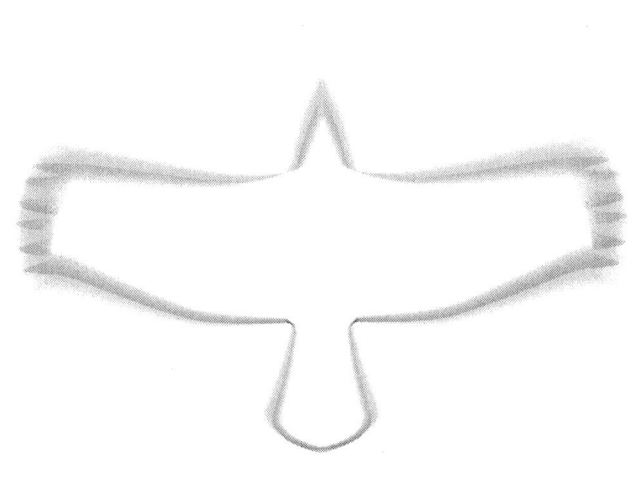

CORE

Hellish life in blank eyes which can't see true.
Finding deep within the core,
The essence of your life.
Keeping life in simple terms unlocks the door.
Keep it open,
Walk in and see yourself you hide.
No barriers,
Free,
No fear.

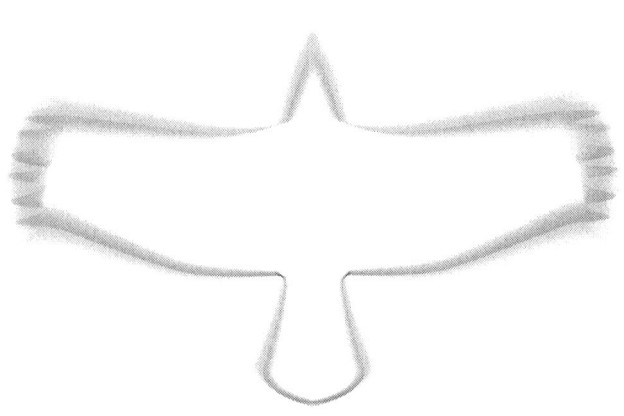

SURVIVAL

Awoken by the subconscious thought spiraling into reality.
Unavoidable factors that make you see the whole picture.
Seeing the most hidden feelings and ideas face to face for the first time.
Keeping it simple and in reality makes a stronger will to survive.
No more to hide,
Will to survive.

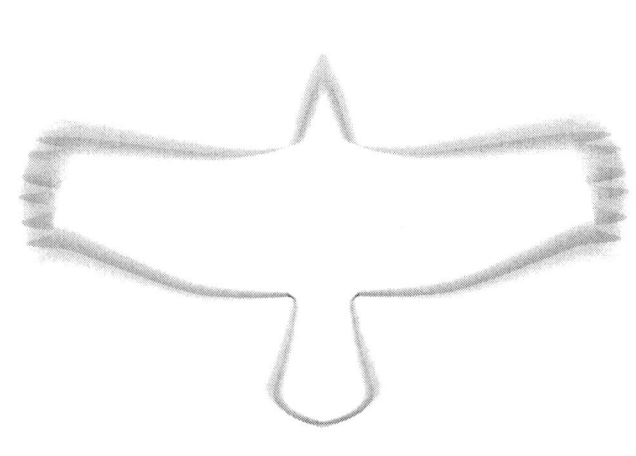

SANITY?

How far can sanity be pushed?
Edge of no control.
Is there a limit to control?
Total breakdown.
Who's the judge of sanity?
I don't know , you tell me.
The control you have has no effect on me.
Freed control is my insanity.
Insanity running wild,
Purity of a little child.
Given back for a little while,
I think I'll go the extra mile.
Push the limit,
Sort the mess.
I like it better I must confess.
Boundaries are set,
Sadness is low.
Wind me up,
Watch me go.
Limitless control breakdown within me,
Freed control is my insanity.

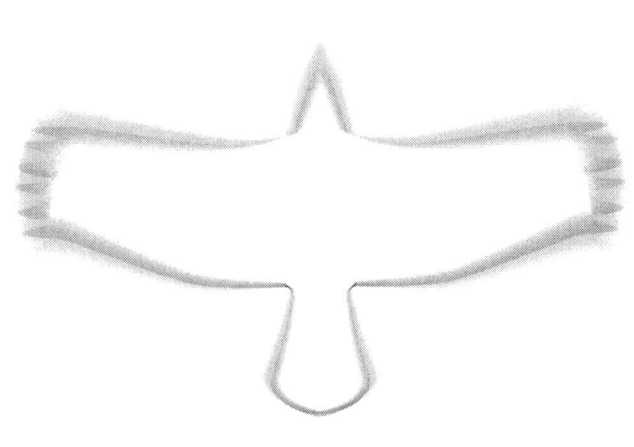

ABSURD

Standing backwards, standing still.
My whole life depends on a pill.
Blank stare, what to do?
Leaning on a window sill.
Attitude is good,
Time to move ahead,
Nothing is happening,
Lying in my bed.
Thinking of all things and never one at a time.
Still I hear everything that is said.
Sometimes scared about going back,
But that's another thought that's in my head.
So much to say but never heard.
Getting frustrated but that's absurd.
Now it's time to move ahead.
Was this said?
Was it heard?
Or are these thoughts inside my head?

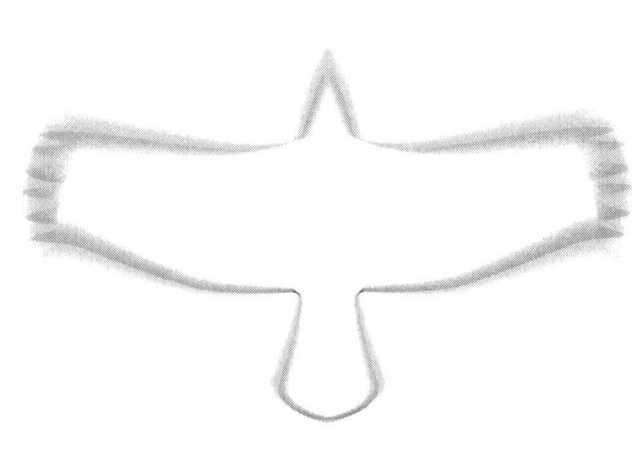

BLACKENED

Blackened mind, blackened soul.
Where do you go to become whole?
Lend me a hand,
Just as well,
Walking around,
Only a shell.
Some kind of help is what I need.
To find a place to replant this soiled seed.
Blackened mind, blackened soul.
Where do you go to become whole?

ADDICTION

Let's begin, let's begin.
Want to know about the biggest sin?
Hurt a man,
Kill his pride.
Stand and pretend you're by his side.
Have the edge, watch his pledge.
Pull the strings inside his head.
Feelings crossing,
Looking straight.
Like a fish that took the bait.
I know these signals,
Know them well,
Sold my soul in living hell.

RED

The releasing of hostility is the end of what I see.
Everything is so blurry and red.
Mixed feelings inside my head.
Need to stop the punishment is my one last mission.
Hurting myself with my own affliction.
Maybe I'm in too deep indeed,
Because I'm scared to death to proceed.
No more frustration,
Hostility,
I can't hear a sound.
I'm moving forward ,
Just don't look down.

FULL CIRCLE

Flat on my back spinning with confusion.
Is this real or just a delusion?
Adding to the pressure,
My ankles tied down.
Always hearing the same profound sound.
How are you?
Does it matter?
Depending on the mood.
High we'll fly,
Low you'll go.
It's something that I don't want to admit or condone.
Everyone with problems is facing them alone.
Open your ears and hear me well,
Sooner or later you'll face your hell.

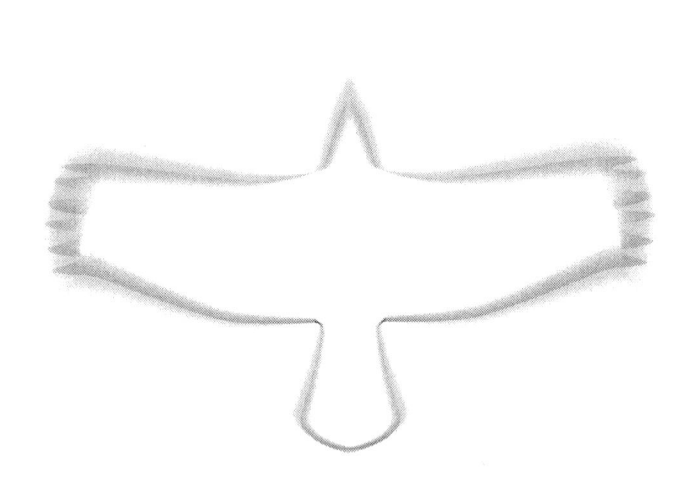

LOST SIDE

Could this be?
That the search was for me?
Illusions were put there to see the lost side.
Put aside,
I thought I died inside.
Awoken by the hungry demon.
Lost side that was hidden before known.
Never shown.
Only grown from the illusion that,
I'm not alone.

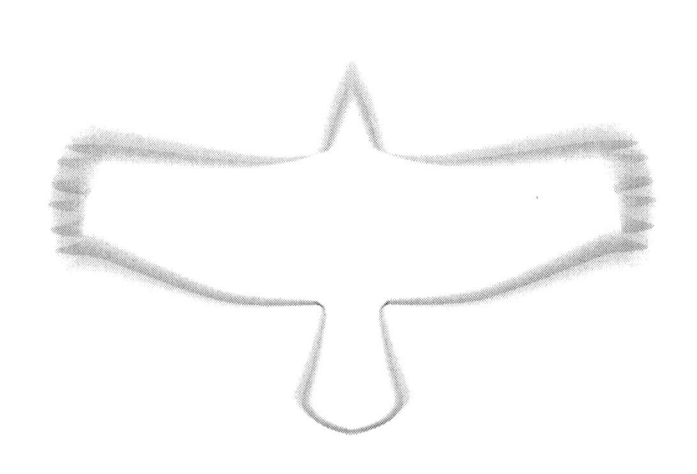

ONE LAST LINK

Chains of life,
Memories link by link.
Remembrance is as strong as each link.
Testing the boundaries,
Always to think.
Breaking apart my one last link.
Shackles of chains of my memories,
Always to think,
Breaking apart my one last link.

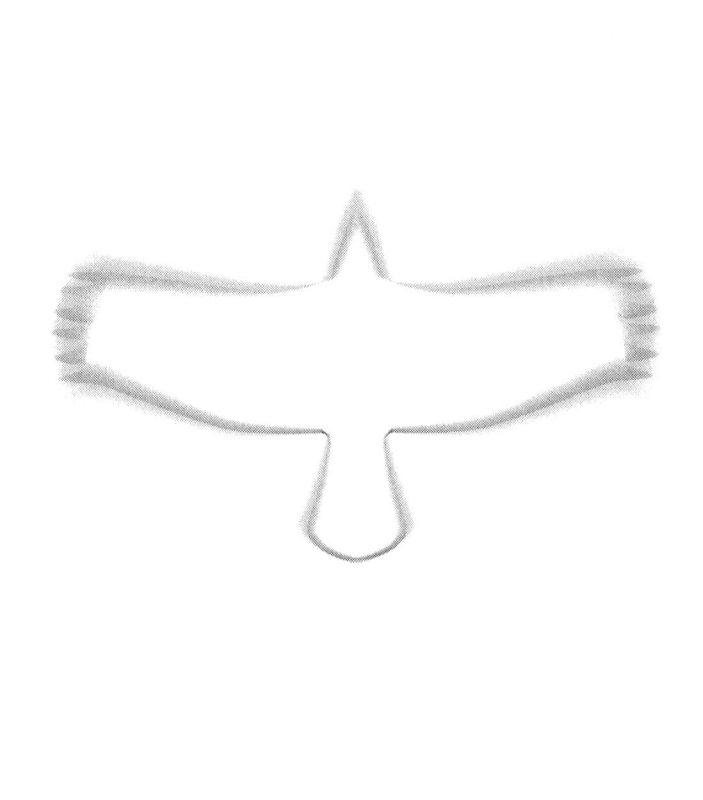

A FEELING

Describing the feeling,
Is it part of the healing?
At least in touch,
Can say that much.
It helps with the dealing,
Of the things that aren't appealing.

11:34

The hands stand still,
When the damage is done.
Slow moving time,
It's already begun.

Purgatory

VOICE

Freedom of choice could be another noise.
Hear my voice,
Could be another noise.
Looking for an answer,
To a problem without a choice.
The road has been already traveled.
Now it's time to walk it and raise my voice.
Looking at a weakness could be looked at like a test. A weakness can be transformed to an incredible strength. I've found if you use your weakness as a gift it can turn out to be a blessing in disguise.

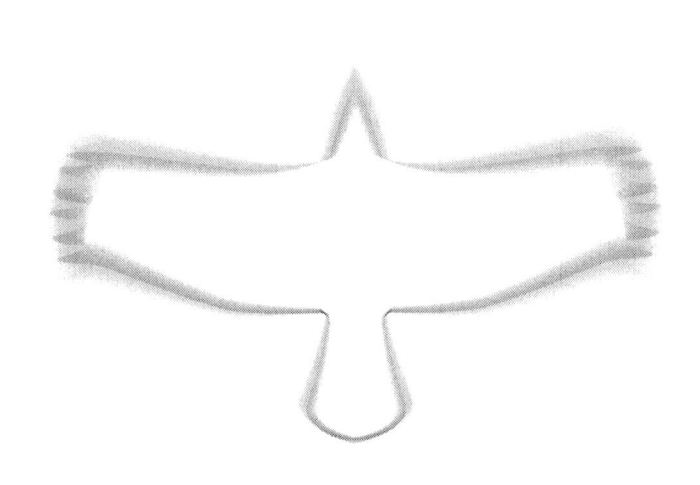

RELEASE

In the dark, freedom is calling.
In the light, tripping and falling.
Looking forward, could be appealing,
In my prayers you will find me kneeling.
Lord above hear my cries for a release,
For only you can give me peace.

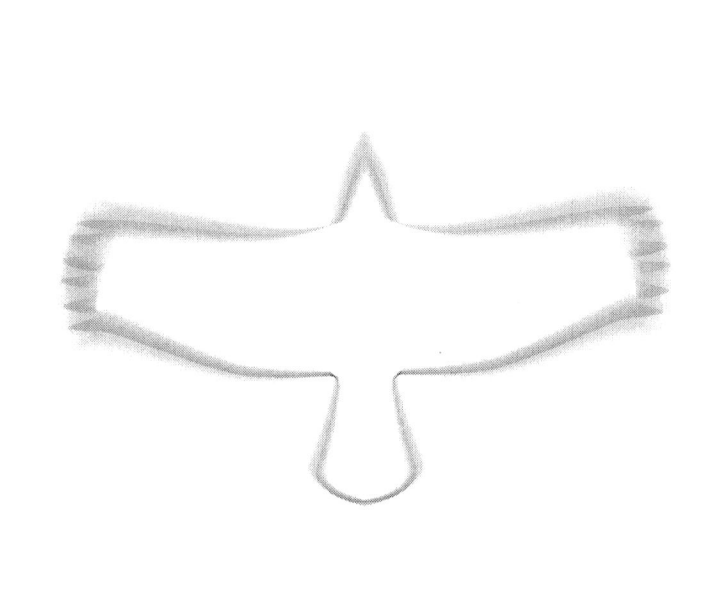

FEAR

Mistaken identity,
Got lost in the clouded perception.
Off balance to a world of off balance ideas and philosophies.
Looking for the missing link which only needed mending.
Mind, body, and spirit,
Which makes a whole person complete.
Living with half and too blind to see.
Running from ignorance,
Keeping the distance from the truth.
Facing the fear of the unknown.

MASKS

Be yourself,
Mask your fears.
Take it off,
Show your tears.
Dying inside,
Covered with pride.
Dark heart holes,
Eventually will sew.
Try to hide the hurt inside,
Spied,
It's not a lie.
Never showing the true feeling,
On your knees it's quite revealing.

CHEMICALS

Always a new surprise without the chemicals lies.
I will not hide, slip, or fall from uncharted flights of grandeur.
Cloudy eyes on sunny days bother me no more.
I'm continuing the journey through the door that was opened in
which the skeleton key will always fit.
Infinite possibilities now that the fire in my heart has been lit.
Ignite the struggle,
Cleanse the impurities.

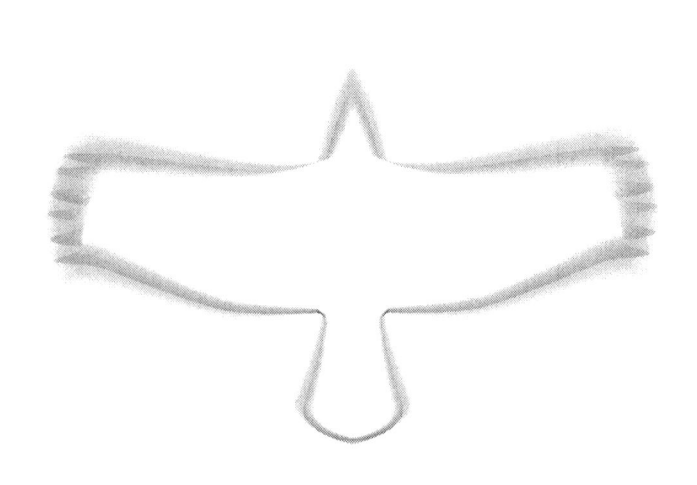

ENLIGHTENMENT

Beautiful thought arises the memories of the angels singing
which showed me my endless goal.
A glowing horizon which warms your soul.
Shown unbelievable ways of thought, understanding, and purpose.
Reborn to grow from the inside out and not start and end at the surface.
Break the surface of deception and ignorance to see what's hiding and screaming for a release.
Releasing and seeing a whole new light.
Instantly feeling an inner peace.
Walking down the tunnel of light with perfect sight.
I took the hard road to get there.
To see is to believe and I have faith in what I see.
The feelings are in my heart if I might go blind to remind me of my faith.
To my delight, I know this is only the beginning of my…

ENLIGHTENMENT.

INDEPENDENT

Independency from the beliefs that were not chosen,
Not settling right, these theories were woven.
Break away from the inconsistent beliefs of someone else's faith.
Be an individual, feeling better everyday.
Follow your school of life,
Never miss a day.
Soon enough you'll see your God,
Then God will show you your way.
Being told what to believe and never to explore,
This can't be the only way so I went to look for more.
Your God can be what you want God to be.
So clear your eyes so you can truly see.
God is not only one I found, although profound that it may sound.
It's deep inside where all those dreams arise,
When you understand I'll see it in your eyes.
When you awake from your dreams and your dreams are reality,
You're beginning to see God and the meaning of immortality.

SCREAMING VENGEANCE

Screaming vengeance for all unheard.
This is your time to be heard.
Speak your voice,
Speak your word.
Screaming vengeance,
I love the sound,
Stand tall and stand your ground.
Bottling up the questions to your goal.
The bottling up binds your soul.
Set forth to get what you need,
You shouldn't have to go out and plead.
Screaming vengeance,
Face to face.
This is the time,
This is the place.
Giving back what I need,
Screaming vengeance was my seed.

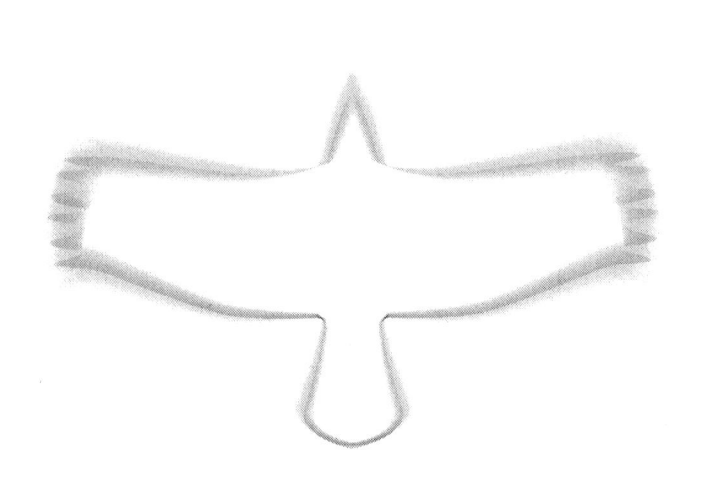

BREAK

To take a break,
Is a break in time.
Let the past be the past unless you want to revel
in it's kind.
Look forward until you find a familiar mind.
You will see the people that are kind.
A break in time.
To remember the kinds of familiar minds.

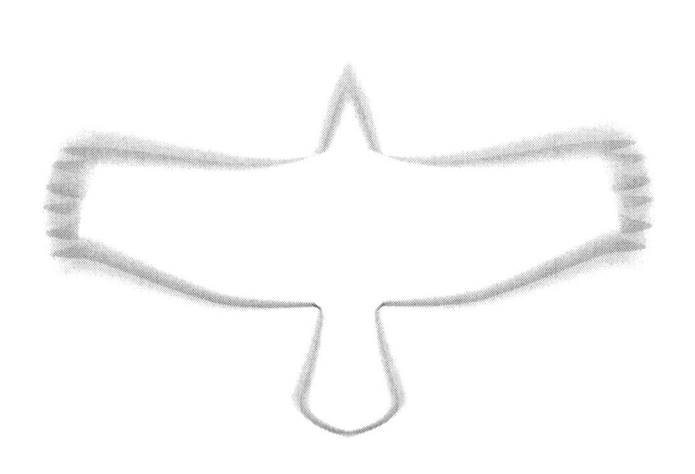

ANGER

The anger has arisen,
Not only in my dreams.
The fear of loss,
For all that it seems.
Shouting is pointless,
Pointing fingers is endless.
How to explain this?
I guess to condense it.
Irrational views,
Paid my dues,
Painful thoughts of endless times.
No one takes kindly to a view from a different mind.

NEW DAY

A new day is dawning,
A feeling of a release.
The sun is out and shining.
In my mind at least with peace.
Looking forward and not so critical,
Ignoring the old and not being so cynical.
Looking for the next sunrise and I know it will be.
Released all the negatives in my mind for the pictures everyone will see.

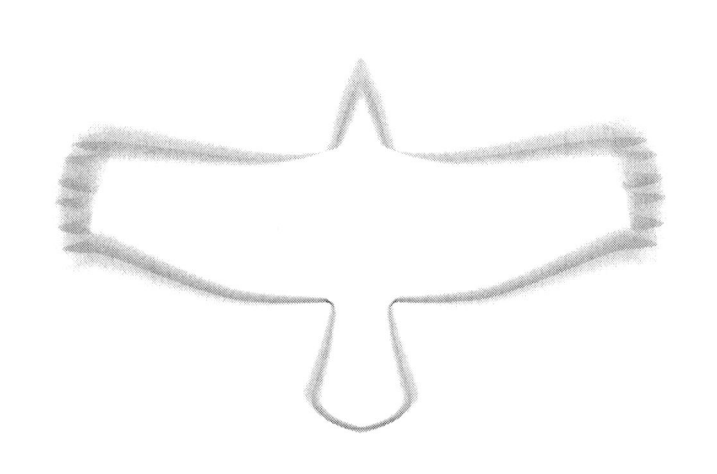

WORLDS APART

A difference between two,
Two worlds apart.
Looking for the reason why this life is so hard.
There are no tangible reasons,
Just differences in the seasons.
Two worlds apart,
Two worlds colliding,
Looking for some reasons,
To stop this world from sliding.

DECISIONS

Decisions are hard when all seems uphill.
Looking toward the sun hopefully to find a time
when my mind will be still.
Seeking guidance from the way of the world,
When the guidance I need are not with my
hands curled.
Lord above hear my cries,
My woes,
My sorrow,
So some day my heart will be filled.

WEAKNESSES

In the eyes that are still,
Can you say the words,
Free will?
Looking to find,
Are the words your kind?
Are your weaknesses your strengths or do your
strengths weaken you?

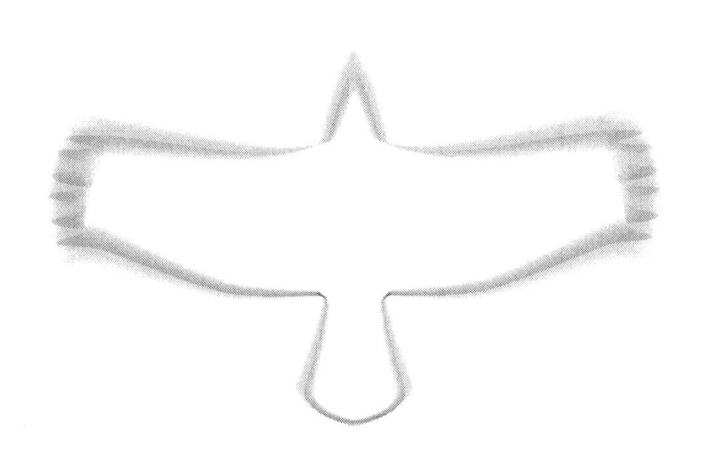

COLORS

The colors seem to fade when I think of this place.
I know it's enough,
I can read it on your face.
Placing these syllables in a sentence for meaning,
When you look into my eyes it's very demeaning.
Let's paint the picture of the perfect place,
So when the colors fade they won't seem to erase.

FOUR WALLS

Why does the sky cry when it's dry?
To open up and cover the earth with it's tears?
To keep people indoors to face their fears?

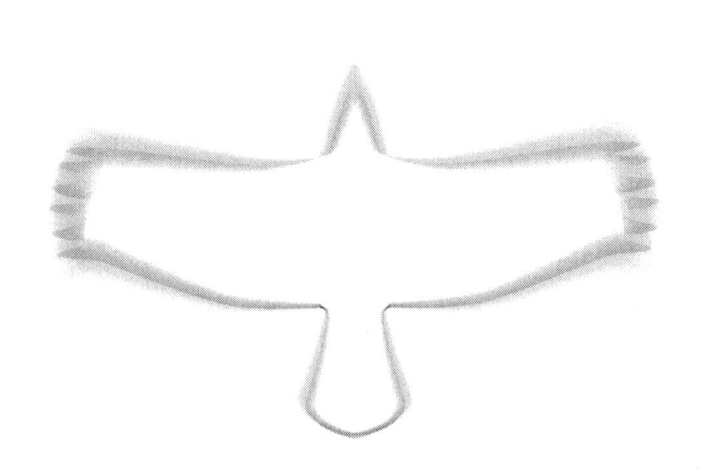

RECYCLED?

We are all started,
Let me begin.
Once and forever,
With original sin.
Are we recycled?
Or are we rejected?
Rejected from a place where everyone has a face.
A face but maybe not a space to exist.
Maybe sent back to resist and exist with,
Original sin.

WHAT'S THE SOURCE?

A sunbeam shines down,
In too deep I might drown.
Look to the sun,
For the battles that were already won.
Living this life,
Looking back,
Was it fun?
Down times,
High times,
Anger does arise.
After this life is there a prize?
Wondering, pondering,
Could there be an answer?
To what question?
What's the source?
Are we living this life with a presence,
A force?
A force that drives to the contest,
The test of life in our daily struggles.
We are pushed by this force,
For life.

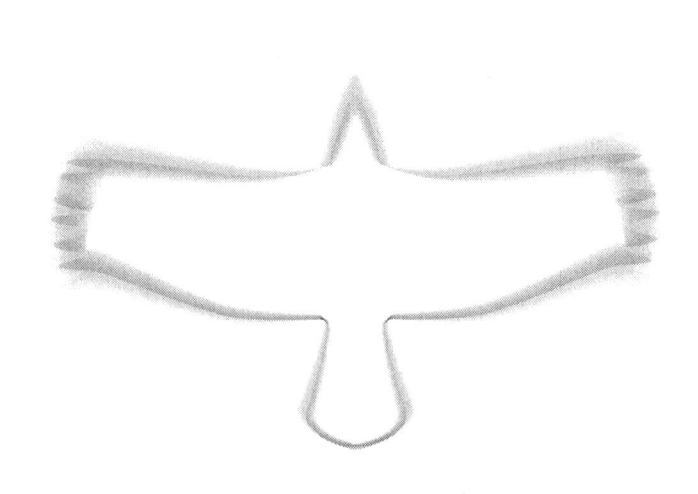

DOOR

Beginning to understand are cries of the unsure.
Many things can change,
Even for the impure.
What is this life and what can possibly be in store?
Look in the soul of a person until you know it's the core.
God wants to show us life and will show us the door.
But it's up to us to walk through and nothing more.
The questions of life are like an eagle which soars,
Freedom is ours if we live life pure.

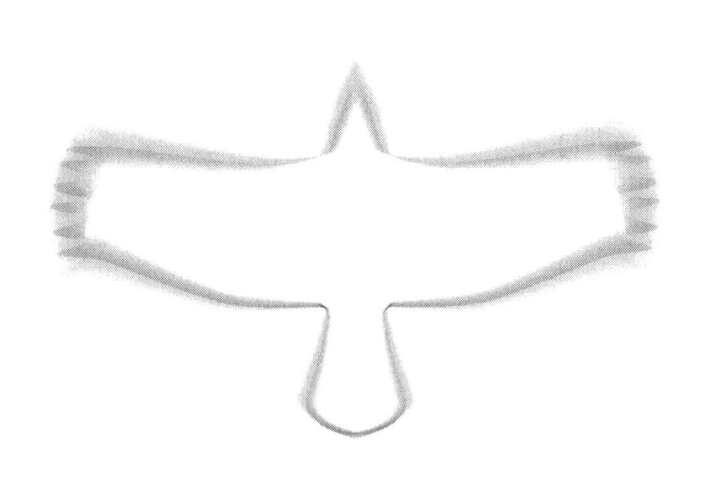

Every time I die,
It's a new beginning,
Of winning,
Or sinning,
I will be born again.

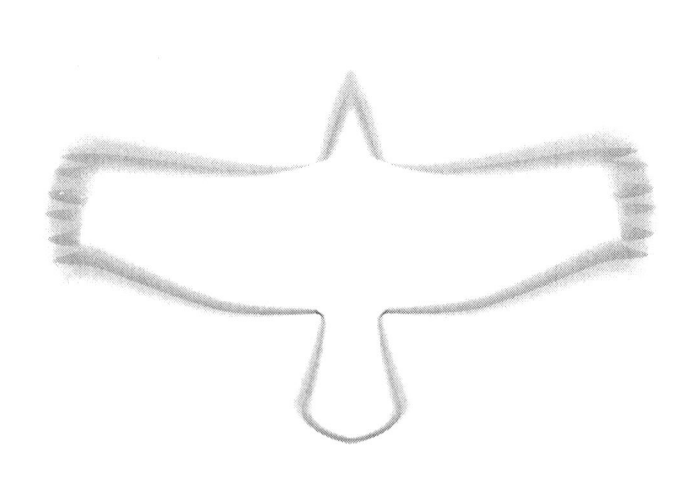

LEARN TO FLY

Need to follow rules,
Rule my life.
Wound runs deep,
Sharp as a knife.
Structure would fall if the rules were broken,
I don't care,
That's my token.
Don't your thoughts come from you?
I don't know,
I hope to know soon.
Looking back it's not too bad.
Hearing the story makes you sad.
Looking ahead it's all speculation,
Tired of the old,
Looking for a new sensation.
Looking at today,
I don't know,
Because I'm looking every which way.
Being a bird and asking why?
Wings are bound and cannot fly.
Answers are left wide open.
Rebuild the structure,
Start over and avoid the lecture.
Being open and free in the open sky,
Open your wings and learn to fly.

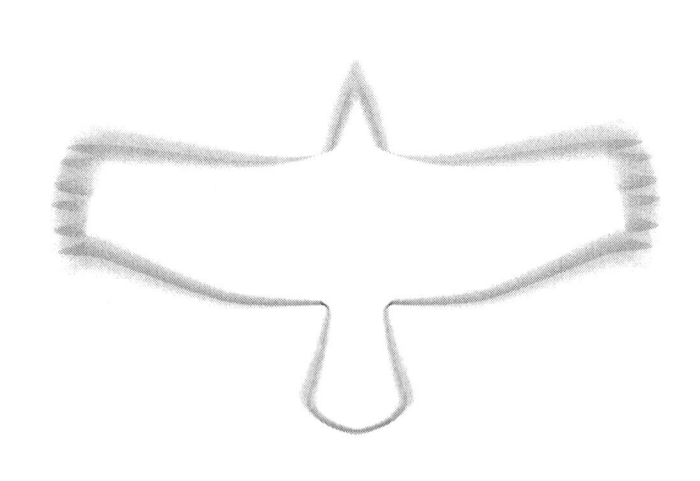

THE QUESTION?

Looking to a time when the time will stand still.
-the judgement
Will it end quietly or will the silence penetrate
the walls and shake furiously?
-the inner walls
Will the fierce light penetrate the soul and shine
like gold or will the residue be like ash?
-the self reflection
Or is this the judgement that was taught?
-the question

About The Author

Jason Insalaco has been in recovery from Bipolar Disorder and addictions since 1995.
His goal in his recovery was to transform his chaotic behaviors and to shine out of his darkness. His path led him to learn about his strengths and weaknesses. Learning this taught him how to cope and structure his life.
Jason is happily married to his wife Tracy and father to his two beautiful children.
In his self acceptance, he has high hopes to break the stigma of mental illness and spread hope for a successful life in recovery.

INSTINCTIVE BIRD™

www.instinctivebird.com

Made in the USA
Middletown, DE
17 November 2017